We Can Teach You to Play Hockey

We Can Teach You to Play Hockey

by Phil and Tony Esposito

with Kevin Walsh

An Associated Features Book

Hawthorn Books, Inc.
Publishers
New York

Designed by Harold Franklin

1 2 3 4 5 6 7 8 9 10

The photographs on pages x, 12, 52, 70, 78, 98, and 112 are by
    Dick Raphael.
The photograph on page 14 is by Ken Regan.
The photographs on pages 38, 47, 64, 76, 77, 88, and 90 (top) are
    by United Press International.
All other photographs are by Joe Black.

To those who taught us the most:

Abbie Naccarato
Angelo Bumbacco
John "Clipper" Lanoce
P. J. Heaney
Our Dad

Acknowledgments

A number of people teamed with us to help make this book. For their contributions we are grateful to Lou Nanne; Matt Ravlich; Jerry Bumbacco; Bob Tomlinson, rink manager of the Memorial Gardens in our hometown of Sault Ste. Marie, Ontario; Fred Sharf, our manager; Joe Black, who took the instructional photos; and Kevin Walsh, who knows what to do on a pair of skates and how to write about it.

P. E.
T. E.

Contents

Introduction

What can an accomplished all-star center who holds numerous team and National Hockey League records still learn about the game of hockey?

"Plenty," stresses Phil Esposito, of the Boston Bruins, at his hockey schools in Weymouth, Massachusetts, Sault Ste. Marie, Ontario, and Richfield, Minnesota, where he teaches young players the techniques and fundamentals that helped him score an amazing seventy-six goals in one season.

"There are many people who have spent years around the game of hockey who think they know everything," Phil points out. "I certainly can't agree on this count because after many years of playing in the NHL I am still learning."

This is one of the bits of reasoning and philosophy that impressed me as I watched Phil and his goaltender brother Tony, of the Chicago Black Hawks, impart their knowledge of the game to youngsters.

"I became a better face-off man in the past few years because I learned something about winning the draw from watching some of the smaller centers like Henri Richard and Dave Keon," says

Phil. "I watched them and decided that I would have to go down the shaft of my stick, sort of like the hitter in baseball who chokes up his bat. That hitter will make a higher average at the end of the season than the home-run hitter with the big swing. The same principle applies to winning face-offs. I know it works because I win more face-offs now than ever before."

Similarly, Tony talks about goaltending.

"One of the best lessons I ever learned came from sitting at home watching television," he notes. "I would watch Johnny Bower guarding the nets, and I'd study how he used his stick to its best advantage."

The Espositos are highly respected as instructors because of their impressive work with young hockey players over the years at their schools and at clinics in the United States and Canada.

There are things they say in *We Can Teach You to Play Hockey* that may differ from what has been taught by others. But Phil and Tony talk from experience as professionals who know what it takes to play and stay in the NHL.

They provide information for the novice as well as for the advanced hockey player. Their instruction is aimed at improving individual skills and techniques whatever one's level of ability and performance.

Phil has written the chapters "The Game," "Equipment," "Skating and Drills," "Shooting," "Passing," "Forward," "Defense," and "The Rules." Naturally, Tony has written about his specialty in "Goaltending"; he also wrote "Conditioning."

The Espositos answer the question: What do you have to learn and do in hockey to be successful?

To make the NHL? Read on.

KEVIN WALSH

We Can Teach
You
to Play Hockey

You know sometimes that net looks like a birdcage.

CHAPTER 1

The Game

The object of hockey is to score goals. It sounds simple, but it's something that takes a great deal of individual skill combined with teamwork. My teammates and I spend sixty minutes every game trying to score goals while somebody like Tony as a goaltender is standing in front of the net trying to prevent goals from being scored.

What hockey is all about is pretty elementary. Everyone is trying to put the puck in the opposition's net. The game is broken down into three twenty-minute periods, and at the end of sixty minutes the team that has scored the most goals wins. If the score is tied at the end of three periods, the game ends as a tie—except in tournament and play-off games, when ties are usually resolved by sudden-death overtime periods, in which the first team to score is the winner. In minor-league hockey the length of the periods and the game is shorter, but the object of the game is the same.

There are six men on the ice for each team when the game starts. The offensive-minded players are the center and his two wingmen. They are the players whose basic job is to score the goals. They are backed up by two defensemen, whose job is to defend against

1

THE RINK

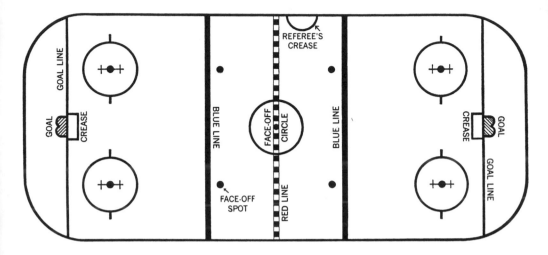

the opposition's attacking center and wings. And then there is the goaltender, whose primary job is to prevent the puck from going into the four-foot-high and six-foot-wide cage at the end of the ice called a net. Its total area is twenty-four square feet, but sometimes it looks as small as a birdcage to the shooters.

I'm sure you have found hockey to be an exciting and hard-hitting game. It's probably the world's fastest sport. The players at the professional level skate at speeds of thirty miles per hour and faster while shooting the puck at speeds up to one hundred miles per hour.

The game is played on an ice surface usually surrounded by four-foot-high boards; this is called a rink. The standard-size rink is two hundred feet long and eighty-five feet wide, although the exact size differs in many NHL cities.

The ice area between the goals is divided into three parts by two blue lines. Each is sixty feet out from a goal line and extends across the rink. Inside the blue line at the end of the ice, where your team is defending the goal, is the defensive zone. Between the blue lines is the neutral zone. Once you cross the opposition's blue line, you are in the offensive, or attacking, zone.

There is also a red line that extends across the center of the rink. It divides in half the center circle where face-offs take place at the beginning of each period and after each goal.

Naturally there are officials who govern the play of the two teams. The man in charge is the referee, and he is assisted by two linesmen. Behind each goal is a goal judge who turns on a red light whenever the puck enters the net. There is also a timekeeper who operates the clock that shows the elapsed time in each of the three twenty-minute periods. A penalty timekeeper keeps the time of the individual players penalized for rules infractions by the referee.

Just as the referee runs the game, a coach runs each team and controls and maneuvers his players. There is never a stoppage of play for substitution in this fast-moving game. When a player gets tired, he comes to the bench, and a replacement jumps on the ice as play continues.

The only times there are stoppages of play are when there has been a rule violation, when a goal has been scored, and at the end of each period, when there is a fifteen-minute intermission.

Our classroom is on the ice.

A craftsman must take proper care of his tools, as Tony does with his mask.

CHAPTER 2

Equipment

Your equipment is designed to provide you with the proper protection while playing hockey. It's your best friend, and it should be cared for properly at all times.

Don't neglect wearing a particular piece of equipment because it feels uncomfortable when you first put it on. Learn at a very early age that equipment that fits properly will protect you from an injury that could put you off the ice for a couple of days, a week, a month, or even longer.

By proper fit I mean something that is comfortable: not too loose and definitely not too tight so that it will interfere with the circulation of your blood.

The skates are the most important part of your personal equipment.

A proper fit on skates is a must. It will help you become a better skater. It's not right to try to skate with skates that are two or three sizes too large. Parents should be reminded of this point. It won't help a young player to learn to skate if he doesn't have a proper-fitting skate boot. An extra pair of heavy socks definitely isn't the answer to getting the boot to fit.

Start dressing with long underwear to absorb perspiration, and be sure to wear a cup for protection.

A garter belt is needed to hold up your stockings.

Put your pants on next.

Shin pads protect your legs and knees.

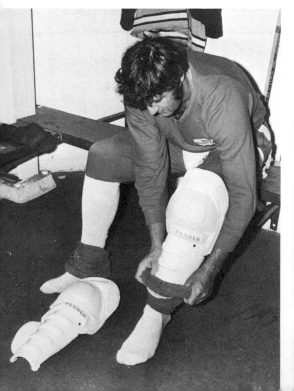

Just what is a proper fit? It's a skate that feels comfortable. Many people insist that the skates should be small. I don't agree. I don't think the fit should be that tight. I prefer to leave a little bit of room for expansion in a youngster. A thirteen-year-old wearing a size 8 shoe would probably get a comfortable fit from an 8 or a 7½ skate boot, but in some cases an 8½ boot might be the best.

You need good support, but I don't feel that kids' feet should be pinched into skates the way we do in the National Hockey League. I wear a size 12 street shoe and a 10 skate. But this isn't good for growing feet.

A lot of people talk about young hockey players having weak ankles. I think you'll find that a proper and a good skate fit will eliminate this problem and make skating that much easier.

As a forward I look for shin pads that are light so that they won't feel heavy and affect skating speed. But the pad must provide protection. It should be made of fiber with a suspension and have a cap to protect the knee. Because they block shots, some

Tape your pads in place but not too tightly.

defensemen wear a heavier-constructed pad for added protection. But a player like Bobby Orr on my team just fills in his pads with cotton for added protection.

The pants should fit properly so they will provide you with protection in the hip, rib, and thigh areas. The pants should hang just above the knee. If the pants are too big or too small, it will be hard to skate in them, and they certainly won't offer the protection they were designed to give you.

Shoulder pads must have a cap to cover the shoulder area and pieces of felt with fiber to protect the arms. Elbow pads are vital.

Skates are tight but shouldn't interfere with proper circulation in your feet.

Shoulder pads are next.

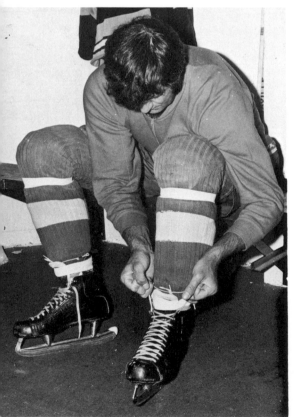

You must protect the bone in your elbow, so a proper fit is very important. The elbow pad will also protect your forearm.

Gloves are designed to protect your hands. They should be properly padded to protect the back of your hand, your fingers and thumb, and the wrist area where you are apt to get slashed. Many gloves have preformed fingers, which afford easy fitting while providing good protection and flexibility.

There are two pieces of equipment that aren't commonly used by players in the National Hockey League but are *musts* for young hockey players—helmets and mouthpieces.

Elbow pads are a must when I talk about proper-fitting equipment preventing injury.

Pull your shirt on, and you're ready to play.

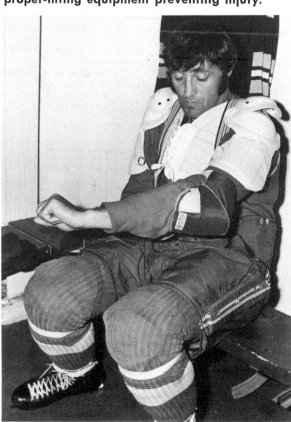

I am very pleased that the wearing of helmets is compulsory at the minor-league hockey level. I think this is great, because a helmet offers you protection at the back of the head, the temple areas, and the top of the head.

I have never worn a helmet at any point in my hockey career, but I can see the day when everyone in the National Hockey League will be wearing them. It will become a requirement under the rules just as professional baseball makes it mandatory for all batters and base runners to wear helmets.

There are many different styles of mouthpieces. The ones I like best are the Pro-Form and the type that can be made by your own dentist. You can talk with it in your mouth and chew gum, and it doesn't affect your breathing. I have used the Pro-Form type mouthpiece, and it didn't affect my breathing at all.

While we are on the subject of equipment, let me talk about proper care. Your parents have spent a great deal of money to equip you properly, so be certain to take good care of it.

All your equipment should be aired and dried after every use. Don't leave it rolled up in a ball stuffed in your equipment bag. And be sure to wipe your skate blades dry so that they won't rust.

Your skates should receive special care. I have my blades sharpened for every game and just about every practice session. You will know your skates need sharpening when you feel them slipping out from under you as you attempt to turn. This means you have lost your edge. Dull skates can be responsible for injuries, so be sure to have your skates sharpened at all times.

How much money is needed to invest in equipment? The skates will be the most expensive item. You can get a serviceable pair of skates in the $20-to-$25 range. The skates professional hockey players use cost in the neighborhood of $75.

The price range for gloves will run from $10 to $40; shoulder pads go from $5 to $25. There are many different styles of pants, and naturally the better they are, the more they are going to cost. Most teams will outfit you with pants, socks, a jersey, and a helmet as part of the standard uniform. This will save you money, but if you have to pay for the uniform, you should figure on spending another $40 to $50.

The cost of outfitting a goaltender is most expensive. The equipment is specialized—skates constructed differently to provide added protection and a mask. The expense is determined by the quality of the equipment. A goaltender could get adequate protection for an investment of $200, but to buy the best of everything, we are talking about $500 to $600.

A youngster must be sure that goaltender is his position before his parents invest heavily in equipment. Here again you'll find that most youth programs will have equipment that can be borrowed for league use. This is probably the best way to start.

The hockey stick is certainly vital. Take care in selecting it. Generally it will have to be cut down. You certainly can't use the same size stick that I use. A general rule for the length of the shaft would be to place the tip of the stick blade in front of you on the floor and cut it off at the point where the shaft reaches under your nose.

The angle of the blade is called its lie. I lean forward when I skate and use a 5½ lie, whereas somebody who skates straight up, like Derek Sanderson, uses a 7 lie.

The lie of the stick, therefore, is selected according to the style of skating that best suits the individual. If you carry the puck well in front of you, you'll want a 4 or a 5, and if you like the puck closer to your body, think about a 6 or a 7.

The goaltender's stick also has lies. A goalie who crouches would prefer an 11 or a 12 lie; a stand-up goaltender will use a 13 or a 14. Again, if you are a youngster, don't try to play with a stick as big as the one Tony uses. Get a lighter stick; it will be easier to handle. If you find that the shaft of the stick is too long, cut it down a bit so you'll be able to control your stick better.

Speed is the most important thing on a breakaway.

CHAPTER 3

Skating and Drills

The name of the game is skating. If you can learn to skate, you can learn to play hockey. As youngsters Tony and I spent all our free time after school and even after supper skating. I can remember eating some nights with our skates on so that we could get right back on the ice.

You can look at the various players in the National Hockey League and see that they all skate differently. Skating style is determined by the physical makeup of the individual.

Most professional players skate with their knees bent, weight slightly forward, and with the movement from the hips and not from the knees.

A good general rule for the young hockey player is to try to develop a good skating stride.

Don't be too erect. Don't walk on your blades. Aim to develop a gliding motion.

The bend in the knee gives you balance and will make it hard for you to be knocked off your feet.

Now lean forward slightly, and push off the inside of your skate blade. Once you are moving, you should be pushing off your back foot while bringing the other foot forward. The harder you push, the faster you will go. Remember, it's the *harder* you push, not the faster you push, that gives you the speed. Short choppy strides should be used only for quick starting.

Now we have you moving in a straight line, but that isn't enough to play hockey. A hockey player must be able to stop, turn, skate backward, and cut both left and right. It won't come easily. This is something that must be practiced for days, weeks, months, years.

I find that most boys can easily cut and turn while skating to the left. It becomes more difficult when they reverse direction and have to go to their right. It is very important that the young hockey player learn to cut both left and right.

To turn, you must know how to cut. When you are crossing over, you keep the weight on the inside leg. Your body should lean

Note how I'm pushing off the outside foot—for power—against the Rangers' Brad Park.

Stopping means cutting the blades into the ice.

toward the direction of the turn. To get speed, you must push off hard with the outside leg, using the inside edge of the blade. You won't have to glide around corners anymore.

Now that we have you moving and turning corners, the next thing is to learn how to stop, or you might spend the rest of your life skating around the rink. When you do skate around the rink developing that smooth stride, try to divide your time equally in both directions. In fact, coaches of Squirt and Pee Wee teams would do well if they had most of their general skating during a practice session or a warm-up done to the right (the hard way) instead of to the left.

There are two ways to stop. The first is with both skates. You lean backward slightly while both your blades push forward and cut into the ice to stop. There is also a one-skate stop. It's similar to the two-skate stop as your blade cuts into the ice. If you want to stop quickly and change direction, something a forward must do almost instinctively, use the front foot. You can also stop on the back foot, which is the best for backchecking purposes. Here all the weight is on your back skate with the other skate off the ice. The free skate swings around in the other direction and gets you moving quickly.

Defensemen must also be proficient in their ability to skate backward and turn while skating in this direction.

Skating backward and skating forward are very similar, but in skating backward your knees are closer together and slightly bent. Skate in a crouched position with your rear end low to the ice. The motion of your hips comes into play now. You move by throwing your body from side to side trying to avoid short choppy strides. Like skating forward, you must develop a smooth gliding motion. Just go straight back using the inside of your blades to push off.

Defensemen must develop maneuverability. They must be able to skate forward and backward skillfully, and they must be able to cut and turn while going in both directions.

If a forward is coming down on your left side, turn your left skate to him, and push off with your right to move in that direction. You just reverse the procedure to cut to the right side. This phase of skating takes time and practice. Don't be impatient if you don't succeed the first time you attempt to cut left or right.

There are many skating drills designed to make you a better skater. They will help you build balance, flexibility, power, and stamina.

When participating in these drills, be sure to go both ways. This is something that separates the true skaters from the ankle benders who glide around corners.

For instance, if you are participating in a stop-and-start drill,

I'm pushing off the inside of my right foot as I start backward.

You get to cut both ways using this drill, and notice how I am carrying the puck with my head up.

be sure to stop left one time and right the next. It's also a good time to practice stopping with two skates on the ice and then just the front skate or back skate.

The important thing as you attempt to develop as a skater is to concentrate on what you are doing. Don't go through the motions. Try to learn and improve every minute you are on the ice. As we said before, skating is the most important part of hockey.

An interesting practice session employs a variety of drills aimed at increasing strength, endurance, and power of muscles while improving flexibility and developing your ability to breathe. At the same time you'll be gaining confidence in your ability to make difficult stops and turns. They'll become routine.

I have chosen some exercises that should help you improve and become a stronger skater. It would help, too, to set up an agility course in which you skate through chairs or tubes. Learn to do this while skating as fast as you can. Then try to skate through the same set of obstacles while carrying a puck. Get somebody to put a stopwatch on you and clock your improvement.

LONG STRIDES
This is the basic stride of all the skaters in the National Hockey League.
The knees are apart, and your body is in a half-squat position leaning forward. This drill is done at moderate speed to loosen the leg muscles and
obtain an increase in the player's circulatory system.

KNEE PULL

Balance is a by-product of this drill. Skate slowly with the stick held shoulder-width. Raise one knee, and place the stick just over the knee. Using the arms and shoulders, pull the knee vigorously toward the chest. Repeat the pull to the chest, then lower the leg, and continue the same exercise on the other leg. Besides developing balance, you will also be stretching the crotch and giving your arms and shoulders exercise.

21

LEG DRAG

Skate at medium speed. Bend one leg at the knee, keeping the other one as straight as possible and trailing behind. Hold the stick at the end and in one hand. Lean over, and point it straight ahead and on the ice. Use the other hand in conjunction with the stick hand to simulate blocking a puck. Make sure to keep the head up, and look ahead. This, too, will aid your balance, stretch the groin, and help develop flexibility.

KNEE BEND
This exercise is aimed at ligament, tendon, and cartilage areas. With the feet fairly close together and coasting slowly, squat down and bounce several times in a deep knee bend. Then alternately move the feet back and forth. Tony says this is an excellent exercise for goaltenders.

23

FEET ON ICE
Begin this drill easily, and build up to an all-out effort. Keep the skates flat on the ice, propelling yourself by a vigorous movement of the ankles, knees, hips, and arms. This will help develop power in your skating.

24

LEG KICK
Skate forward slowly. Hold the stick about arm's length and chest level. Kick one leg and then the other to touch or attempt to touch the stick. Be sure to keep the leg as straight as possible.

LEG SWEEP
Balance, flexibility, and maneuverability are developed with this exercise. Skate backward at a moderate speed. The right leg is brought straight up, swung to the left, and returned to the ice on the outside of the left skate. Repeat with the left leg, bringing it straight up, swinging it to the right, and returning it to the ice on the outside of the right skate. This exercise is done in a slight crouch position.

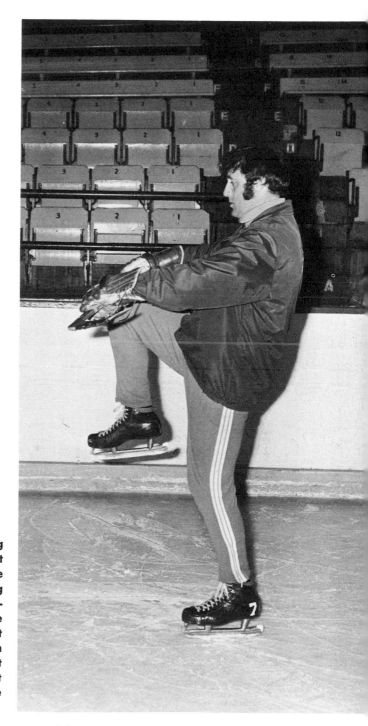

KNEE LIFTS
Begin this exercise skating slowly in either a straight line or a circle. On the whistle alternately bring up legs so the thigh is approximately parallel to the ice and the lower leg is at a right angle to the thigh or upper leg. Be sure not to bring up the skate so it is in the rear or under the seat.

RUNNING SIDEWAYS

This is a good team drill that will help build endurance along with power and maneuverability. You begin this exercise at one end of the ice with the players on the left side. On the whistle they run to the right on a slight angle toward the other end of the ice. Keep the skates flat on the ice and the body facing straight ahead. On the whistle change directions to the left. Make sure you face straight ahead or to the end of the rink you just left. Don't look in the direction you are moving.

PUSH AND PULL

A partner is needed here. The drill helps to develop power, strength, and endurance. You line up facing each other with one player pushing the other down the ice. The player being pushed should offer resistance by angling his skates to form a snowplow. It will take hard work to move your partner. He'll do the pushing coming back up the ice. You can also pull each other by locking arms, or with the aid of a hockey stick skate backward pulling him down the ice. Again, resistance can be added by placing skates in a snowplow position when you are being pulled.

Push-ups

CHAPTER 4

Conditioning

Conditioning is all-important because hockey is such a fast-moving contact sport and the body must be ready to stand up under the extreme stress and strain.

With the regular playing season, Stanley Cup play-offs, and the hockey schools, Phil and I are on the ice ten months of the year.

I myself don't wait until the opening day of training camp to start preparing for the season. I start working out on my own a week or two before we report to camp, sort of training for training camp, so that I'll be ready when the coach blows his whistle and starts us to work.

A young hockey player must develop his body. We are not big advocates of weight lifting, but we do feel that special attention should be paid to the development of your wrists, forearms, and legs.

Sit-ups, push-ups, and chin-ups are good off-ice activities that will help condition your body. Sometimes some of these drills can be done on the ice, too.

A favorite wrist-strengthening drill of forwards is one where you attach a weight to the end of a rope that is secured to a cut-

Sit-ups

Stretching helps to loosen muscles.

33

Always be certain you are warmed up before playing in order to avoid needless muscle pulls. We warm up for fifteen minutes before a game.

down broom shaft or other suitable handle. Now with your wrists and hands practice rolling the weight up. Do this every day.

Running in the off-season will help develop your leg muscles and at the same time help in your breathing.

When training camp starts, don't overextend yourself the first day. Remember that some of the muscles are being used for the first time in weeks. Take it slowly for the first week or ten days. Work to be in top condition when the season opens.

If you are not physically prepared for the hitting part of the game or if you attempt to go too hard at the beginning, you'll find yourself on the injured list, and an injured hockey player isn't much help to his team.

Be sure to loosen up before the start of a game. In the National Hockey League we go out on the ice for fifteen minutes prior to the start to loosen up muscles. Your muscles must be loose. If they aren't, you'll develop pulls and tears that will have you sidelined.

The sticks are an obstacle course, and the goal is to run on your skates to improve balance and agility.

Every hockey player should pay special attention to his diet. Eat nutritional foods, but don't eat a big meal or drink a lot of milk just prior to a game or practice session. If you are inclined to put on weight, watch your diet. Extra weight slows you down and reduces your effectiveness.

Goaltenders must develop strength so that they will be able to spring back up on their feet when they are down on the ice blocking a shot. They should also work on building strength in their stick hand. I usually recommend grasping a goaltender's stick at the knob and, while standing straight, lifting the stick to shoulder height and returning it to the floor. Repeat this several times.

Stick-hand strength is a must for a young goaltender. While standing straight lift your stick from the ice to shoulder height. Keep repeating.

Pick your spot before you shoot as I did here against New York's Ed
Giacomin.

CHAPTER 5

Shooting

Before we talk about slap shots, snap shots, flip shots, and wrist shots, let me give you the most important word in shooting—quickness.

The different types of shots are used for different situations. To me it really doesn't matter what kind of a shot you take as long as it's quick and on the net. You want to catch the goaltender by surprise.

I use what I call a snap shot, which I learned from Bobby Hull while I played in Chicago. It's something in between a wrist shot and a slap shot.

I like it because I can get the shot off quickly. I usually catch the goaltender moving with this quick shot, and it has resulted in many goals for me over the past few seasons.

Young hockey players should work hard to develop a good wrist shot. You won't need a slap shot until you get older and stronger. Besides, you can be much more accurate with a hard wrist shot.

The shooter has to pick a spot. When you are shooting on net, look where you are shooting. Know where the goaltender is before you fire.

There are four corners of the net. The best spot to pick is the spot with the most net showing. Generally a low shot is the hardest for a goaltender to handle.

Work on firing shots to the low stick side and then to the low glove side. It's a bit harder to stop a shot to the stick side. The same is true if you decide to fire high. A shot on the high stick side is far more difficult to stop than a shot to the high glove.

Most goaltenders have good glove hands and will handle all shots that come up in the glove area, so unless this is the only opening when you look before taking a shot on net, it should be your last choice. Again, the element of surprise makes for the best shots in hockey.

To develop a hard shot, you are going to have to practice and

I just sweep the puck along the ice and follow through low, making a wrist shot.

do your exercises for developing your wrists. While you are prac-
ticing your shot, learn to shoot the puck without looking down at
the puck on your stick. Glue your eyes on the spot where you want
the shot to go, and you'll be surprised at the accuracy you'll develop.

When you shoot, you slide your lower hand about halfway down
the shaft of the stick while gripping firmly. This gives you more
power.

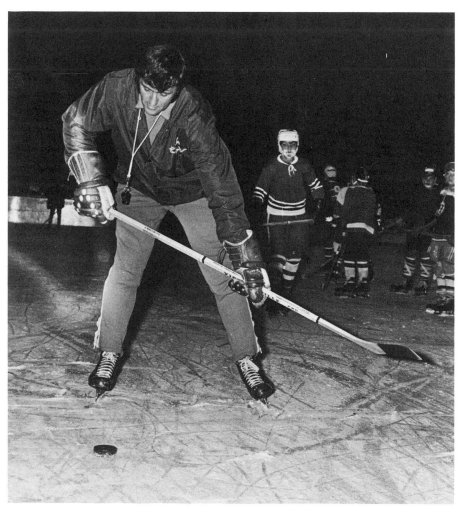

Slide your hand down the shaft a bit to get more power in your shot.

My weight is pushed off my left side as I shoot for power.

For a wrist shot the puck is on the middle of the blade. The stick is slightly cupped, and you put your entire body into the shot. When shooting the puck, the weight shifts from your back skate to the front skate and then you follow through. When you are actually firing the puck, all the weight should be on your front foot. You simply sweep the puck forward and snap your wrist to let the shot fly.

You have your head down when you take a slap shot just like a golfer trying to hit a golf ball. A slap shot isn't too accurate, and for this reason its use should be limited.

When you get a shot, make sure it's on the net. It can't go in unless it is, and for this reason I don't recommend a slap shot for young hockey players.

The slap shot is similar to the wrist shot in that the key is putting your body behind the shot while shifting weight from the back skate to the front skate. In the backswing of the slap shot the stick comes quite a bit off the ice, and as you shoot, the stick strikes the ice just behind the puck.

The backhand shot uses the same shooting theory as the forehand shot. The wrists are cocked ready to fire, the puck is posi-

Keep your eye on the puck when making a slap shot.

The backhand shot is the same as the wrist shot with the same weight shift from the back foot to the front foot.

tioned on the heel of the stick, and the weight shift is from the back skate to the front skate.

The follow-through for the backhand shot as well as the forehand shot determines the height of the shot. To get off a low shot, don't break the wrists coming through the shot, and be sure to follow through low.

The flip shot, something that is very useful around the net when you must lift the puck over a fallen goaltender or just to pass the puck over a stick to a teammate, is different in that the puck is positioned out on the toe of the stick and you flip the wrist in a lifting motion as you follow through high. It's a difficult shot to master but very handy.

But I still like my snap shot, which is halfway between a wrist shot and a slap shot. I like it because I have shot it before the goal-

The puck is on the heel of my stick as I get off a backhander against the Rangers.

48

wrists up quickly so the puck will come straight up.

tender knows the puck is coming at him. The puck is shot from the middle of the blade, and like the other forehand shots, the weight shifts from the back skate to the front skate. It's the quickest shot in hockey.

Like everything else, this is something that doesn't just happen. It takes a lot of practice to master a shot like this. Even now, after using the snap shot in the National Hockey League for many years, I still spend an extra half hour on the ice after a practice session working on this shot. I have Ken Hodge, Wayne Cashman, or some other player feeding me the puck from the corner, and I work to improve my shot.

The harder and quicker your shot is, the more goals you will score. And, finally, don't overlook accuracy. Remember that a shot on net, whether it's hard or weak, has a chance to be a goal, whereas a hard shot that is wide of the net can never be a goal. It's just a loud noise off the boards or the glass.

Taking my favorite snap shot, you see that my feet are in position and my eye is on the puck. When the puck hits my stick, I'm shooting it in one quick motion.

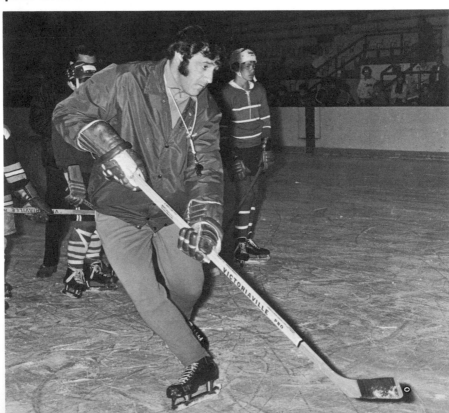

I can see who's open as I prepare to pass with my head up.

CHAPTER 6

Passing

Keep your head up while you are carrying and passing the puck. You have to see where you are going and what you should be doing with the puck.

Like other facets of the game, passing and stickhandling take particular skills which are developed through repetition. The ability to give a pass and take a pass is essential.

As a centerman I must be able to carry the puck and hit my wingmen with passes to keep the attack going.

One rule that must be emphasized in passing: Always lead your man. Pass to the spot where you think your teammate's stick will be as he breaks up ice at full speed. Don't pass it *to* him; if you do, you'll find you are passing in his skates all the time. I try to lead him so that he skates into the passed puck. I don't want him to have to break his stride.

Making a forehand pass is a lot like shooting a wrist shot. It requires a long sweeping motion of the blade of the stick along the ice. Don't slap at the puck. The blade of the stick should never

Just slide the puck along
the ice making a pass.

leave the ice. If the stick does leave the ice, you'll find that the puck will, too, and it will be that much more difficult for the receiver of the pass to control the puck.

Passes should be made firmly—soft passes are often intercepted —and never pass the puck to a man who is covered.

The pass is made to a player's stick, so if you are on the receiving end of a pass, be sure to have your stick on the ice ready to catch the pass. This also serves as a target for the player making the pass.

When the puck is coming to you, the blade of your stick should be cupped slightly, and as the puck hits your stick blade, relax your grip slightly, and let your stick give a couple of inches to absorb or cushion the impact. By doing this you'll find that the puck won't skip over your blade. Reverse the procedure to catch a pass on your backhand.

Notice how my stick is cupped as I prepare to receive a pass. When the puck hits my stick, I'll relax my grip slightly to cushion the impact.

I use the same sweeping motion for a backhand pass.

I keep my stick on the ice to hide the puck from the goaltender on a drop pass.

The backhand pass is very similar to the forehand pass in that it's a sweeping motion. Be sure to keep the follow-through of your blade along the ice so that the pass will slide smoothly in the direction of your intended receiver.

The fact that you must give forehand and backhand passes while skating up the ice means you should always carry the puck in front of you as you skate. If you develop the bad habit of carrying the puck on your side, you will be able to pass the puck in that direction only. You must learn to slide your passes in both directions.

There are times when you must lift a pass over a defender's stick. This is called a flip pass and is accomplished by moving the puck on the toe of the blade, and with a slight lifting motion of the wrist, you will be able to lift the puck over any obstacle. Just rotate your wrists upward.

The drop pass seems to be becoming more popular. There are two types of drop passes—one where you just leave the puck for the trailing winger and one with a tail that you slide back as you skate toward the net.

Generally, when making a drop pass, you should just leave the puck for your trailing teammate. Keep your stick right along the ice to hide the puck, and then move in the direction of the net so that you can screen the goaltender. By doing this you'll also find yourself positioned perfectly to pick up rebounds in front of the net.

Stickhandling is an art. I have spent a great deal of time learning how to handle the puck. For years I used a straight-bladed stick when I was playing center ice with the Black Hawks. Then, players like Stan Mikita and Bobby Hull started to play with curved sticks.

I used a curve-bladed stick in practice for an entire season before I ever attempted to use the hooked blade in a National Hockey League game. In the old days before the rules regulated the hook you were allowed to use, some of those sticks started to look like bananas.

You should keep both hands on your stick and keep it gripped firmly in your hands so that it can't be knocked from your grasp

Your thumb and fingers grasp the stick firmly.

by an opposing player. The pressure of holding the stick should be provided by your thumbs on one side of the shaft and the tips of your fingers on the other side. Do not try to crush the stick with the palms of your hand. Hold it mostly with a grip provided by your thumb and forefinger. This will give you more feel.

The position of the stick is important. You must always be ready to take a pass, shoot, or steal the puck, so for this reason the stick should always be near the ice surface. If you carry the stick above the ice level, the puck may be by you before you get the blade of the stick back on the ice.

Remember to keep the stick in front of you. This is where the puck is going to be, and that's where your stick should be.

I always carry the puck well in front of me as I skate up the ice. I have a long reach, so I use a 5½ lie stick. The closer you skate to the ice, the lower the lie of your stick. I really have it out in front, whereas players like Derek Sanderson and Johnny Bucyk skate with the puck closer to them and use a more upright 7 lie stick.

While skating up the ice you are usually moving the puck from side to side; this is called dribbling. You cup your stick from side to side as you move the puck, setting up a defenseman with your moves. A more skilled player will also dribble the puck back and forth instead of side to side, giving the puck to the defender, hoping to get him to commit himself, and then quickly pulling it away to break around the defenseman.

Stickhandling must be done with your head up at all times. You can imagine the amount of practice that is needed to develop this talent.

I said earlier that you should never carry the puck on your side while skating up ice. The only time the puck and stick would be in that position is after you have faked your way around a defender. In such a situation it is permissible to carry the puck to the side. Use your body to shield the defenseman from the puck, and at the same time you can move in on the goal and be in excellent position to take a shot at the net.

Let me clarify one more point. You should basically skate with two hands on your stick, but there are times when one hand is permissible. If you are on a breakaway, you don't need two hands on your stick. Push the puck ahead of you with one hand, and work to get quick skating speed needed to skate in alone on the goaltender.

One more secret. I said that you should keep your head up at all times so that you won't lose sight of everything that is going on around you. Even the professionals, however, peek at the puck once in a while. But they don't drop their head to do it. They just lower their eyes for a quick look and only when they are not quite sure where the puck is.

Swing the puck wide, and when you get a half step on the defenseman, cut right for the net, and make your shot.

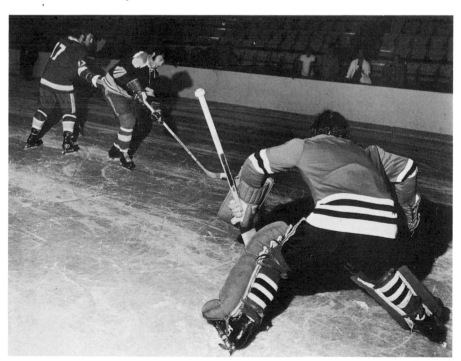

Use your body to get position on the opponent when playing the puck as I have done here along the boards against Walt Tkaczuk.

CHAPTER 7

Forward

The job of the center and wings during the course of a hockey game is certainly more than to just go out and score goals. Forechecking and backchecking are basic duties that in many instances will determine whether your team leaves the ice the winner or the loser.

Many hockey experts will tell you that games are won and lost in the corners, and it takes hard work to control the puck when it gets in the corner.

Forechecking, a duty of the forward, is the attempt to break up a play in the opponent's end of the ice before it starts. Who does the forechecking depends on the team's style of play.

The wing can do the forechecking, the center iceman can handle the situation, or the first man into the attacking zone can do it.

I play center for the Boston Bruins a little differently from many of the other center icemen in the National Hockey League because of wingmen like Ken Hodge and Wayne Cashman, who skate on my line. Cash and Hodge do the forechecking for our line, and

If you miss the puck forechecking, be sure to play the man.

I back up the play or move into the slot area in front of the net. I'm the shooter on our line.

This style of play is a bit revolutionary. I believe it started when Jean Béliveau was in his prime and was used successfully by Stan Mikita and a few others like myself. In most other team systems the center will do the forechecking. Derek Sanderson is an outstanding forechecker as a center. He uses a sweep check effectively while pressuring the other team in its own end.

There are other times when the first man into the end handles the forechecking duties.

It doesn't matter who is doing the forechecking; you always approach your man on an angle. You try to play the puck, and if you miss, you can at least take the man out of the developing play by stepping into him with your body. Don't let him advance with the puck on the play. If he does, the second man, the backup man, moves in quickly to play the puck.

If the puck carrier is swinging around the net, you cut him off as he attempts to come out and drive him toward the boards.

Forecheck with your stick extended in front of you. Don't be looking directly at the puck. Look at the man; you'll still be able to see the puck.

If you are close to an opposing player as he goes for the puck in the corner, go right with him, and make an effort to control the puck and set up a potential scoring play with one of your teammates.

Backchecking is usually the job of the wingmen. But if the wing is caught deep in the attacking zone, the center must pick up the open man. Backcheckers help make the defenseman's job easier and certainly limit the scoring chances on your team's goaltender. They say a forward should go down the ice as fast as he can and backcheck faster. This is certainly a great idea.

When you are backchecking, always keep near the man you are covering. It's best to try to keep him between the boards and yourself. Stay just a bit ahead of him but not so far ahead that he'll be able to shake free by cutting in behind you, and always remember

I look at the man, and I can still see the puck while forechecking.

to keep your stick in front of you. If a pass comes in his direction, you'll be able to block it if your stick is on the ice where it belongs.

Follow your check all the way to the net if you have to. Just be sure the player you are checking doesn't come up with the puck uncovered in the slot area. If he does, you haven't done your job.

If in our defensive zone my team gets control of the puck and then loses it, I feel it's the job of the wings to cover the other team's defensemen out at the blue line. This is called covering the points. Some hockey people think differently, but I feel it should be played this way because it's difficult for a center to go back and forth to watch both points.

Whereas backchecking is primarily the job of the wingers, taking the face-offs is almost exclusively the job of the center. You must develop a quickness in the face-off circle, and the only way to do this is to develop strong wrists and practice taking the draw as often as you can.

The most important face-off on the ice is the one that comes in your defensive zone. You must stop your opponent from winning the draw here. If you don't, there's a chance that it will result in a goal for the opposing team.

I always try to draw the puck against the man I'm facing. I even draw it back toward my own net if I feel that the center opposite me is going to draw the puck toward the boards. Many people disagree with me on this point. But I always tell my goaltender to watch for a shot because I'm going to try to draw the puck back.

If my opponent is a left shot and the face-off is in the left circle, the most natural way for him to draw the puck is toward the boards. There are only three or four centers in the NHL who can draw the puck on their forehand.

I just want to go against my man. I try to outguess him. I watch his feet to see how he sets up. This will usually tell me if he's going to draw the puck back or try to take a shot at the net. I find if the left foot is close to the line that extends from the face-off spot and he's a left-handed shot, he's going to shoot. If the right foot is closer to the line, he'll be drawing it back. I guess it's a little bit like the hitter in baseball trying to guess what kind of pitch the opposing pitcher is going to throw next.

Before I move into the face-off position I always make sure that everyone on my club is in the proper position. I position my feet first, and before I put my stick on the ice I look at the other center's feet to see what he's going to do. Don't put your stick on the

I'm winning the draw back to the point against Jean Béliveau.

Be ready to take the face-off when you put your stick down, and always watch the official's hand.

ice until you are set in a comfortable stance because as soon as you put your stick down, the official is going to drop the puck.

I choke down on the shaft of my stick a good three or four inches. I feel that the lower I go down the shaft, the better, because it seems to give me better leverage and more quickness. The baseball batter who chokes up on his bat gets his bat around quicker, and I feel that the same principle applies here.

I have only been choking up on my stick in recent years. I never did it before, and I never won many face-offs either.

Now that I'm ready I look at the official's hand, and as soon as he makes his motion to throw the puck down for the face-off, I'm moving my stick at the puck.

What do I do after the puck is dropped? If I win the face-off, I try to get myself in position to start a breakout play. I'll be twenty-five or thirty feet in front of my net with my stick on the ice ready to take a pass. If I lose, the opposing center has either taken a shot off the face-off or drawn the puck to the side or back to the point. In this case I stay with my man, being sure to spoil any scoring chances that come his way. I have to cover him in front of my goaltender, being sure to lift his stick off the ice.

As I said before, quickness is important. I have been winning 70 percent of my face-offs the last two years. Some nights you are sharper than others.

I can remember one game, a 4–3 loss to Chicago. I scored all three goals for the Bruins and won every face-off I had with Stan Mikita that night. Everything I did was right.

A few weeks later we were playing the Black Hawks again, and I didn't win a single face-off.

It seems that the little center icemen give me the most trouble on face-offs. I didn't have any great problems with Jean Béliveau before he retired or top centers like Alex Delvecchio and Jean Ratelle. They are all big.

But guys like Henri Richard, Dave Keon, and Vancouver's André Boudrias are closer to the ice and just a bit quicker. They give me a great deal of trouble.

There are certain face-off situations that must be treated differently. In the attacking zone I'll try to get the puck back to Bobby Orr or one of the other defensemen on the point. Or I'll try to move the puck in the direction of one of my wingmen. There are times when I try to shoot on net, and I sometimes use my skates to advance the puck toward the net, hoping to get off a shot from in close.

As I said before, the important face-off comes in my team's defensive end. For example, time is almost out, my team is protecting a one-goal lead, and the face-off is next to my net. This is a very vital situation, for in most instances the opposing team will have pulled its goaltender in favor of an additional forward.

Under these circumstances I don't care where the puck goes when it's dropped. I just make sure my man doesn't beat me clean

I'm shooting off the face-off as I use my foot to kick the puck clear and then shoot.

on the draw. I take a quick swipe at the puck and step into the opposing center.

I move my stick underneath his. If you place your stick on top of the opposing center's stick and he's stronger, he'll go right through your stick and take a shot.

HINTS

I feel that the center should be the smartest player on the ice. He must know everybody else's job and be able to step in to cover an opening if another player is caught out of position.

A winger's job is to stay in his lane; by this I mean if we were to divide the rink into three equal lanes, the right wing's job would be to go up and down the lane on the right side of the ice. He should seldom leave his lane. The wing must forecheck and backcheck and be ready to cover the point on defense if the defenseman on his side of the ice has rushed the puck into the attacking zone.

Centers and wings both must be able to give and take backhand and forehand passes.

It is becoming more common to see wings playing their off-wing, like Wayne Cashman, who is a right-handed shot playing the left wing on my line. If I pass the puck a little behind Cash, he can reach back a bit and take a shot on net in one motion. And he actually has more angle to shoot on the net because his stick is more toward the center of the ice. When I break down the ice on a one-on-one situation, I like to know the defenseman I'm skating down on. If he is tall, has a long reach, and has his stick out in front of him as he skates backward, I'll try to make him commit himself by trying to poke check the puck off my stick.

When coming down on any defenseman, I'll come up to him, say five or six feet, throw a couple of head and shoulder fakes— dekes, they're called—hoping he'll react in one direction so I can go the other way.

Here I want to be sure my opponent doesn't win the draw. I'm tying him up as I move into him. I didn't try to win this face-off.

If the defenseman doesn't move, then I have to make the first move. Now what I do will depend on where I have the most room to operate against the defender.

If I'm coming down ice on the defenseman and he's in the middle of the ice, I'll make a move with the puck to my left and pull it back to my right. This is the natural way, the easy way, for a left-handed shooter.

I keep a mental book on the defensemen I play against, which is something you should probably do if you play in a league where you face each team more than once or twice each season. I know which way the defenseman can turn best, so I work on his weak-

Against Roger Crozier I fake him left, draw the puck to the right, and flip in a backhander as I finish off a breakaway. Notice how he made the first move.

ness. Conversely, a defenseman should have a book on rival forwards. He should be able to pick up a forward's move if he uses the same fakes every time he breaks down the ice. Once you have him figured out, play him accordingly.

When I have a clean breakaway, the first thing I do is look at the net. If the goaltender is way out of the net, I'll probably fake him. But if he's out and starting to move back into the net, nine times out of ten I'll shoot.

It's simple: If the goaltender is out of the net farther than he should be, fake him, and if he's moving back into the net, shoot the puck.

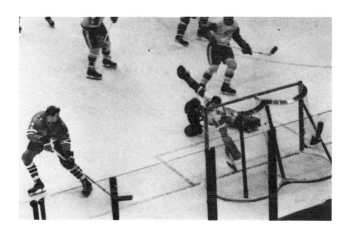

I never take my eyes off the puck.

CHAPTER 8

Goaltending

I have always been a goaltender. When we were growing up back home in Sault Ste. Marie and started to play hockey in the neighborhood, I was in the nets.

In organized play I started as a goaltender in minor-league hockey, and I have played at every level on the way up from junior to college to minor pro and right on into the National Hockey League.

The days of pushing the goaltender's pads at a young hockey player and telling him he doesn't skate well enough or he's too fat to play any other position but the goal are over.

Perhaps I'm a bit prejudiced in my thinking, but the job of the goaltender is most demanding, and the contribution the goalie makes to the team is vital. Being a goaltender is a pressure job. It's like the catcher in baseball and the quarterback in football.

I feel that a goaltender has to be in top condition. He must practice as hard as a forward and should be able to skate as well as the forward.

Don't pay any attention to people who tell you anybody can

Like a forward, I wear underwear to absorb perspiration. I have added a large piece of cotton under my cup as an extra cushion.

My pants go on next.

Knees are exposed to shots, so I wear special knee pads.

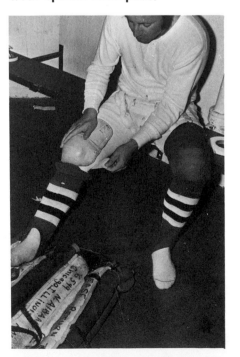

play goal. It takes quickness, good reflexes, a lot of hard work, and plenty of courage to become an outstanding goaltender.

Everybody seems to think goaltending is a two-hour job. Well, it's not. During the season it's a full-time job. Remember, anybody can have a bad game. If a wing has a bad game, nobody notices it, but if a goaltender is having an off night and plays poorly, everybody knows it.

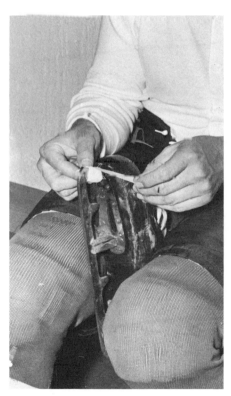

Tape around the front of the blade will save your straps from being cut.

I put my leg guards on now while I still have freedom of movement. The widest part of the pad is on the outside of my leg.

There is a lot of pressure on you if you've decided to play goal. The day of the game I'm nervous all day. I'm always afraid I'm going to do a bum job.

You should start playing goal when you are young. I'd have to say that the first major requirement would be to develop your skating. The skating is the key, so don't be afraid to step out on the ice and play forward or defense in a pickup game. I did this when I was young, and it really helped.

I know I am a good skater. You'll need such skating ability to develop balance on your skates. You have to be able to move from side to side quickly. If you can't move your feet, you'll soon learn that you will always be getting beat on the low shots.

There are a couple of styles of goaltending. I prefer to play more like Glenn Hall than Jacques Plante. I like to go down a lot

This is the easy way to get the lower straps buckled.

Now it's time to tuck my chest protector into my pants.

to block the puck. There is nothing wrong with going down to stop a shot.

Plante is a good goaltender, but he is a stand-up netminder. I don't like the stand-up style myself because I feel you get caught out of position too much. Instead of backing into the goal, you're moving out of the net as the shooters approach. When you move out and they make a pass across the net, I feel you give the pass receiver an open net to shoot at.

I try to play the angles on the shooter. I believe in starting out beyond the crease area and then backing in as the shooter approaches—the way Hall or Roger Crozier do it. It's a new approach to goaltending.

When I was younger, I was a stand-up goaltender. I feel I could still play that way, but I think I'm more effective playing my up-

Shoulder pads protect the goaltender's arms, too.

I pull on my shirt, and I'm ready to play.

and-down style. I call this aggressive goaltending. You attack the puck.

The other way you are playing the percentage. As I grow older, I may have to adjust to the stand-up style because with age you start to slow down physically. A guy nearing forty certainly couldn't play my style. Hall did and was very effective, but he is a very strong man.

I try not to tell young goaltenders too many things at once at our hockey schools and the different clinics I give during the course of the year. However, there are three basic areas a young goaltender must understand if he is going to become good at it.

First, he must learn to play the angles. You can't play the position properly by standing on the goal line. If you do, you give the shooters too much net to shoot at. Be on the outside edge of the crease area when you are making a save. When you back into the net, you are just making it hard on yourself.

If you get out at the top of the crease, cutting down the shooter's angle, you'll find that many shots are going to hit your body. You don't have to do a thing. The puck just hits you, and you have made the save.

To play the angles properly, you'll have to develop a picture of where you are at all times so that you won't be caught out of position.

The second basic is skating. I hate to repeat myself on this point, but I feel it's important to the proper playing of the position. You must have the ability to move in the net, and if you can't skate, you certainly won't be able to move.

The third basic is an ability to size up the situation that is facing you in a split second. But try not to anticipate a shot. You don't want to commit yourself. Make the shooter make the first move.

Be comfortable when you are standing in the net. Weight should always be on the balls of your feet, the glove should be hung comfortably at your side, and your stick should be on the ice. Keep your stick blade straight. If it's tilted on an angle, the puck will sometimes hit it and deflect into the net.

Move out of the net to the top of the crease to cut down the angle. If you back into the net, you'll give the shooter a lot of net to shoot at. You can see the difference in these two pictures.

I'm comfortable waiting for the shot. I have the weight on the balls of my feet, my stick on the ice, and my glove at my side. I'm ready for the shot.

Some say you should keep your legs close together at all times, but I think that this not only makes you uncomfortable but limits your mobility.

You have to be in a standing position where you have good balance. I like to play with my legs wide apart. My advice is to do what you feel is comfortable.

When taking the stance you want to be in when the shot comes, you must bend your knees—don't lock them—and move your rear end back so that you are sort of in a rocking-chair stance.

Keep your eye on the puck at all times. As I said before, try not to move before the shot is taken, and once it is, do anything you can to stop it.

It's perfectly all right to go down on the ice. Just stop the puck the best way you can. Stopping the puck is your number-one job. But one word of warning: Don't be down on the ice when the puck carrier is approaching the net.

The glove is a very useful tool of the trade. Catching the puck is a good thing because it prevents rebounds. I always try to play my body behind my glove when I have time. The puck can do funny things. It can go up, down, or sideways, and if you just use the glove and the shot dips and breaks off your hand, the puck will be in the net.

Keep your glove hand at your side. I keep it right against my side so the puck won't break off my body or arm and slip into the net. I like to hold my glove about knee high and wide open. As soon as the puck hits it, I snap it closed quickly.

Use your stick to your advantage. The use of the stick by the goaltender is the most underrated aspect of playing the position.

I'd say right now that I'm one of the best in the NHL at using the stick. Gilles Villemure and Ed Giacomin with the Rangers are good, but most of the other goaltenders don't seem to use their stick at all.

I picked up this phase of the game watching Johnny Bower play for Toronto on television. He used his stick for years and is by far the best poke checker I have ever seen.

Any goaltender can use his stick to poke check. You can't use it

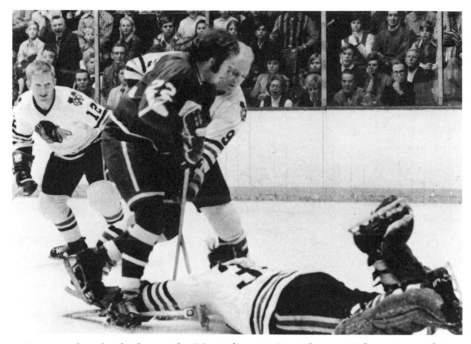

When I poke check the puck, I just dive at it with my stick as I am doing here against Garth Rizzuto, who is being tied up by Bobby Hull.

when the guy is skating directly at you. You use it when a puck carrier is cutting in on the angle and he tries to deke his way around you.

You dive at the puck to poke check. Be sure he commits himself to cutting around you, and as he does, use your judgment on when to move and dive in front of him, hitting the puck with either your stick or your body while knocking it free of his stick. This is something that takes practice but is very effective, and I always stress it when instructing young goaltenders.

Also work on clearing the puck. You must be able to lift it over an opponent's stick and fire it into the corners of the rink. This is something that takes strength.

Practice shooting the puck with your goalie stick. Be sure to use a stick that is the right weight for you. Certainly, a young goalie shouldn't be using a stick like mine. If it's too long, cut a piece of the shaft off, and if it's too heavy for you to handle, pick out a junior model.

When you make a save, you don't always have to clear the puck. If there is any doubt about your ability to clear the puck, fall on it. Don't ever leave a loose puck in the crease area.

But if there is time, clear the puck to the corner, or if you catch it and want to leave it next to the net for your defenseman, just drop it outside the post, and be sure it's a few inches behind the goal line. This is something you can work out with your defensemen. Find out where he likes the puck, and when there is time, you can set up the puck just where he wants it.

Your main job is to stop the puck, however. Make the save and then worry about rebounds and clearing the puck to the corner.

Be sure to hold the goalpost when the puck carrier is in the corner. Keep your foot inside the post, and have your stick ready to deflect the puck when it's going to be passed out from the cornor or from behind your net.

If the puck is going out front, you can be sure an opposing player is out in the danger zone, the slot area in front of the net. Do anything to keep the puck from going into the slot area.

HINTS

There are times when you have to come well out of the net to play the angle on the shooter. The only time you can really afford to get caught out of the net is when the puck carrier is cutting in on you and your defenseman is right with him forcing the play. The puck carrier doesn't have time to deke you; he can only shoot, so you play the angle.

If you stay back in the net in this situation, you give him more net to shoot at. When you move out on the angle, there will be nothing to shoot at but your big pads. When he takes a shot, the puck will hit you. If it breaks through you, it's your fault.

If a puck carrier is breaking in alone on you and he has a lot of

Notice how I have my left skate inside the post and I'm using my stick in an attempt to block Jean Ratelle's passout. Both are important fundamentals.

To move across the net from post to post, I turn my left skate in the direction

time to make his play, there are a couple of ways to play him.

The first way is to stay in the crease. When you do this, he's usually going to shoot the puck.

The second way is the way I play it. When he breaks down the ice, I'm approximately five feet outside the crease, and when the puck carrier looks up as he approaches the blue line, he sees he has no net to shoot at. Now I have him thinking about deking, and as he approaches the net, I back in slowly.

I try to force him into trying to deke me as he moves in close, and once he commits himself, I have to move to stop the puck.

If there is time, I slide over, but if there isn't much time, I'll dive to get there any way I can in order to block that puck.

You dive between the puck and the net, not to a specific spot. Dive right at his stick so that you are close to him. He'll really have to get his shot up quickly to score.

want to go and push hard off my right foot.

This is how I play shots to the four basic shooting spots:

Low stick

Low glove

High stick

High glove

Work on skating backward and forward in the crease. And practice going from side to side. To go from post to post across the goal mouth, turn the lead skate in the direction of the far post, and push off hard with the behind leg.

A goaltender must learn to drop and flop. But more important he must learn to get up automatically. This is something that takes strength, so it will be hard for you to master this until you get a little older and stronger physically. But work on it because it will give you quickness.

Always be sure your teammates line up properly for a face-off in your own end.

As a goaltender you should study the opposing shooters in your league just as the shooters should try to learn the weakness of the goaltender. Some say I can be beat on high shots because I go down, whereas Jacques Plante can be beat low. They say Glenn Hall is weak on high shots, too, because he goes down, but from the records I keep I get beat on the low shots more often than I do on high shots. This might be a good message to shooters. Keep your shots low.

But I have found that the good shooters in the NHL aren't as concerned as much about high and low shots as they are in making you commit yourself. They want you to move first. Phil is one of the great waiters. He usually holds the puck until the goaltender moves.

I always talk to my teammates during a game. I encourage them and let them know where an opponent is or when they are going to get hit so they can brace themselves. I yell if there is somebody in front who is uncovered, but I'm not just talking for the sake of talking. I'm trying to help, and for this reason I feel that a goaltender must know what is going on at all times. He must know the forward's and the defenseman's jobs.

I'm very concerned about opposing players who park in front of my net. Scorers are very dangerous when they are five or ten feet out where they can get off a good shot or deflect a drive. I want my defensemen to force them out of this area. If the players happen to be big like Phil, the Mahovlich brothers (Frank and Pete), or Gordie Howe (now retired), I want the defenseman to

Have both legs on the ice when you slide to block a shot. Try to avoid having one leg swinging in the air.

Practice sliding in both directions as I have done here with Jerry Del Giudice. You'll notice he has room for improvement.

get their stick. Certainly, I want my defensemen to bump them and give them grief, but they are all rangy, and if you don't get the stick, they will still make a play on the puck.

In a one-on-one situation I want the defenseman to steer the puck carrier to the corner and preferably onto his backhand. I don't want the defenseman to screen me, and I don't want a direct shot taken from the slot area. I don't want the defenseman to touch the puck. I just want him to play the man.

On a two-on-one situation we work together. I want the defenseman in the middle of the attacking players, backing up slowly. When they move in close, say fifteen feet, I'll usually shout *Now*, and the defenseman will spring quickly at the man with the puck. This forces the puck carrier to make a quick decision. He will either shoot fast or make a hurried pass. If he shoots, he probably won't get off his best shot, and I'll be at the top of the crease cutting down his angle while blocking the shot. If he passes off, the defenseman stays with the man who had the puck, and I play the man to whom the puck was passed.

As I said, this is something I have worked out with my teammates so that we are prepared and tuned in when we are faced with these types of situations.

There isn't anything wrong with dropping to block a shot. But be sure you spring back up on your feet after you stop the shot.

Bobby Orr is the defenseman who has changed the game. Notice his powerful stride as he moves toward the puck.

CHAPTER 9

Defense

The role of the defenseman has certainly changed since Bobby Orr arrived in the NIIL. Teams have started to think about a defenseman becoming a more prominent factor in the offensive style of play. General managers and coaches are looking for defensemen who can skate and get the puck out of their own end. They are looking for defensemen who have the ability to trigger an attack.

It takes a great deal of ability to do what Orr does on ice. He adds something to the Boston attack with his ability to relieve pressure in the defensive end by rushing the puck up ice. Bobby has such great acceleration that he quickly becomes an offensive threat. Add his great shot, and you can see how a defenseman contributes offensively to a team.

But everyone who laces on skates isn't an instant Orr. A defenseman can play like Orr only if he has tools like Bobby. How many do?

Basically I feel that the defenseman's job is still defense. He must keep the opposition in check while limiting the other team's scoring opportunities.

A defenseman's role is vital to the success of a team, and there are general areas where special skills are required of the defenseman in order for him to do his job properly.

A defenseman must be a very strong skater. Naturally he must skate backward with the same ease that he skates forward, and he must develop balance and the ability to cut both ways to play the attacking player.

A defenseman must develop a hard shot on net, keeping in mind that all shots from the blue line must be kept low. If your shot takes off from out on the point, you won't find too many forwards on your team standing in front of the goaltender screening him. And more important, if the shot is high, you reduce the chance of a teammate deflecting the shot. Tony will tell you that one of the hardest shots to block is the one that changes direction just in front of the net, and the easiest is the high shot he catches with his glove. So be sure to work on your shot, concentrating on keeping it low and hard.

A defenseman must learn to use his stick as an extension of his arm. It can be used to poke check and sweep check the puck off an opponent's stick.

To poke check, hold the stick in front of you as the opposing player skates down on you. When he comes close enough, just give a firm jab with the stick at the puck on his stick blade, and knock it free. You should take a step at the player while making this play. Let the man come to you, and don't commit yourself too soon or he'll give you a deke and go right by you. Montreal's J. C. Tremblay is one of the best at poke checking.

The sweep check is a dangerous maneuver that should be used very sparingly by young hockey players. It's a judgment move which, if it fails, will allow the attacking player to move right by you. You let the man come to you with the puck as you do in poke checking, but you try to approach him from an angle, and when

That's Minnesota's **Lou Nanne** poke checking the puck off my stick.

The sweep check

he gets near enough so that you can reach the puck with your stick extended flat on the ice, quickly sweep the puck off his stick.

Certainly, many hockey players have developed reputations as hard-hitting defensemen with their checking, and this seems to be the part of the game defensemen enjoy most. But before we get to the different checking methods, we must discuss the various rushes that will come in your direction during the course of a game. You must learn to read and react to these situations.

The one-against-one rush calls for you to play the man and not the puck. You must be skating backward as the puck carrier comes

A one-on-one calls for the defenseman to play the man. Lou Nanne isn't going for the puck. He is about to step into me.

A two-on-one situation requires the defenseman to stay in the middle of things while hoping to force the eventual shooter off the angle.

down the ice. If you are standing still, it will be easy for him to go by.

Don't watch the puck—concentrate on the man. Look the puck carrier in the chest. His chest goes everywhere his legs will take him, and you won't go for fakes he is throwing with his head or shoulders. Try to make him commit himself first and then you move in on him, or, better still, stay between him and the net, and force him off the shooting angle. It's advantageous to force him on to his back hand so that even if he does manage a shot, it will be a weak shot on your net. As a goaltender Tony wants the defenseman to steer the man off the angle. He doesn't want a screen shot or a shot from the slot area. There is no way he wants a powerful shot taken.

The two-on-one situation calls for the defenseman to stay between the two attacking players while trying to force the puck carrier off the shooting angle. If you stay in the middle, it will be hard for the puck carrier to make a lateral pass to his teammate. Once the puck carrier is off the angle, it's the goaltender's job to play him.

Two against two is similar to the one-on-one situation. It's a man against man with the goaltender concentrating on the puck carrier. Don't make the first move. Just be sure to be skating backward, and don't try to check the man with the puck unless you are certain that you will be able to hit him. If you miss, a two-on-one situation develops in your defensive end, and your partner will be caught out of position.

Three-on-two is the most difficult rush the defenseman faces. It calls for the two defensemen to work together, and you attempt to have one defender play the puck carrier while the other covers the attacker who is in the most dangerous scoring position. Make the forwards commit themselves first. They will usually make either a lateral pass or a drop pass. Again, it should be your aim to force the shooter off the angle. Backchecking forwards can help you decide who should be covered in this situation.

Another important duty of the defenseman is to cover in front of the net in the defensive zone. If you are the right defenseman and the puck is in the left corner, your partner should be playing the puck in the corner, and you should be in front of your net covering the attacking player in the slot area ten to fifteen feet in front of your net. Know where the puck is and where your check is at all times.

Use your stick to lift his stick off the ice. Always lift the stick up. If you try to lean on his stick, he may overpower you and manage to get a shot off. But if his stick is in the air, he'll have trouble handling even a passout from the corner.

When you are properly positioned in front of the net, you'll be able to clear rebounds, intercept passes, cover opposing players, and body check a puck carrier if he tries to skate out from behind the net and take a shot at your goal.

Judgment is needed to decide when you should release from covering a man in front in order to check another attacking player who is trying to skate out from behind the net or the corner. This is a key play for you because you don't want to let the man walk in alone on your goaltender at any time.

Remember, if the puck is on your side of the ice, you play the puck, and it's your partner's job to cover in front of the net.

As you can see, this area is one of the defenseman's chief responsibilities.

Now for body checking: This is a skill that takes practice and perfect timing. You can use either your shoulder or your hip to hit the puck carrier, and I think you'll find it rewarding when you catch an opposing player carrying the puck with his head down. Just step right into him. He'll never see you coming and probably won't know what hit him.

But you don't have to knock him down hard for a check to be considered successful. You have checked your man if you have taken him out of the play.

You must remember that by the rules you are allowed to take only two steps when checking a man, and you can hit an opponent

When covering a man in front, always be sure to keep your stick under his. Notice how Lou has tied me up a bit more by putting his stick between my legs.

107

(Above) On a shoulder check the defenseman just steps
into his man. (Below) If they catch you with your head
down, they'll give you the hip.

only if he is carrying the puck or is the last man to have touched the puck.

When you shoulder check the puck carrier, he must come within your range. When he does, you move your shoulder solidly into his chest while shoving hard off your rear foot.

The hip check is most commonly used along the boards. You bend low, and when the puck carrier comes within range, you step into him pushing off the outside foot.

A defenseman must learn to block shots. There are two ways to block a shot. In close you just drop to your knees using your body

Throw your body at the puck to block a shot.

When you are away from the net, you can drop to one leg, and then you'll be ready to break up ice if you deflect the puck in front of yourself.

to block the shot aimed at your net. This takes some courage, and you will have to develop the proper timing so that you drop as the shot is being taken.

The other way to block a shot is with one knee on the ice and one hand free of your stick trying to deflect the shot in front of you. If you do this, you'll be able to spring to your feet and quickly break up ice. This method is used primarily when you are well away from the net. In close you just do the best you can to stop the opposing team's shot.

Another important lesson for a defenseman is, don't ever give up checking a puck carrier even if he has you beat. When you keep trying, the puck carrier knows he has to rush and won't get as good a scoring chance as he would if you just quit and thus give him a lot of time going in on your goaltender. That would put the goaltender at his mercy.

If you stay with the man, it helps the goaltender to play the shot. It will allow him to move out of the net to work the angles. There is no way a goalie can do this if the man just walks in alone.

Offensively work hard on your passing. The quickest way to take the pressure off your team is to head-man the puck to a break-ing forward and let the other team's defensemen worry about who's covering whom or blocking shots. Certainly, to become a well-rounded defenseman, you will have to be able to pass the puck and stickhandle just as well as the centers and wingers.

The referee controls the game.

CHAPTER 10

The Rules

Naturally, in playing with the Bruins, we use the professional rules of the National Hockey League, and this is the set of rules under which I feel everyone should be playing.

Rules are a very necessary part of the game of hockey. They are something you will have to learn to live by as a hockey player. And, of course, the first thing to do is buy a rule book and study it.

There are five basic penalties:

1. Minor (two minutes)—for hooking, tripping, boarding, spearing, slashing, roughing, holding, cross-checking, butting, high sticking, charging, elbowing, and delay of the game.
2. Major (five minutes)—for fighting or when a minor infraction is committed with deliberate intent to injure the opposing player.
3. Misconduct (ten minutes)—for use of abusive language to an official, but this is a penalty against the individual and not the team, so the team doesn't play shorthanded.
4. Match (balance of game)—for a deliberate attempt to injure an opponent. Team plays shorthanded for either five or ten

minutes. Length of penalty is determined by the severity of the injury.

5. Penalty shot—a free shot on the goaltender is awarded to a player who is pulled down from behind on a clean breakaway when there is no opponent between him and the goal except the goaltender. The penalty allows him to skate in alone from center ice with only the goaltender to defend against the shooter.

Tripping

Elbowing

Hooking

A lot of people talk about fighting in hockey. It's a major penalty. Fights happen, and I don't agree with fighting in hockey. But they happen because hockey is a body-contact sport played at a very fast pace. I really don't know what measures can be taken to stop fights, although the rule they introduced at the start of the 1971–1972 season has helped to cut down on the mass brawls. It calls for the "third man" intervening in a fight to be thrown out of the game and fined one hundred dollars.

Holding

117

The minor and more frequent penalties are judgment calls on the part of the referee. But most of the penalties are picked up by lazy or stupid hockey players.

Take hooking and slashing penalties, for example. They usually result when you are chasing a player, trying to check him off the puck. If you skate a little harder and make up the stride or two that you are behind the puck carrier, you won't be picking up needless penalties that hurt your team.

Cross-check

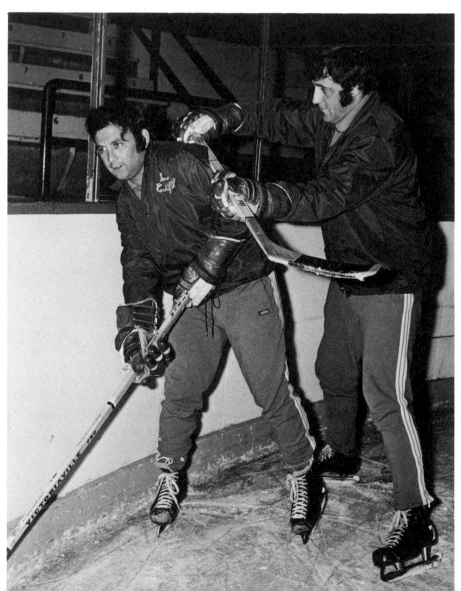

Slashing

High stick

Basically you must know and understand the rules of icing and off side. They are rules designed to keep the game controlled and moving.

Off sides hurt your team because they happen while your club is in control of the puck and on the attack. There are two types of off sides in professional hockey. The first type: You are off side if a pass from a teammate crosses two lines before it reaches you. An example would be your defenseman passing you the puck from inside his own blue line across the red line at center ice to a point near the other team's blue line. This is a two-line off-side pass because the puck has been passed over a blue line and a red line onto your stick. It calls for a face-off from where the defenseman made the original pass.

The second type of off side: A player can't precede the puck into the attacking zone. The position of the player's skates, and not that of his stick, is the determining factor in deciding an off-side call. A player is off side when both skates are completely over the outer edge of the determining blue line or in the case of a two-line pass, the red line.

A good player learns to straddle the line as he moves up ice so he won't lose momentum waiting for the puck to cross the line. This is something you should work on. Learn to cut at the blue line, being sure to keep one skate behind the line.

The rule on icing reads:

> For the purpose of this rule the center line [red] will divide the ice into halves. Should any player of a team, equal or superior in numerical strength to the opposing team, shoot, bat, or deflect the puck from his own half of the ice, beyond the goal line of the opposing team, play shall be stopped and the puck faced off at the end face-off spot of the offending team, unless on the play the puck shall have entered the net of the opposing team, in which case the goal shall be allowed. For the purpose of this rule the point of last contact with the puck by the team in possession shall be used to determine whether icing has occurred or not.

Spearing

So you can see that you can hurt your team if you needlessly ice the puck. The face-off will come all the way back to your end of the ice next to your net.

Certainly, there are times when your team is in trouble in its own end, and it's best to relieve the pressure by firing the puck the length of the ice. You'll develop judgment for doing something like this as you pick up playing experience.

I have talked about professional rules here, but some leagues will use the National Collegiate Athletic Association (amateur) rules that govern high-school and college play in the United States, and still other leagues play under International Rules.

The NCAA rules differ from professional rules in that there is no red line to speak of and no two-line off sides. Checking is prohibited in the attacking zone, and I feel this is one rule that has hindered the development of the young American player.

When a player can't get checked in his own end of the ice, he starts carrying the puck with his head down. This is a bad habit.

The International Rules have a red line for the purpose of checking. A player can hit only in his defensive half of the ice.

Besides limiting the hitting part of the game, the International Rules call for an automatic whistle for icing as soon as the puck crosses the goal line at the far end of the rink. Nobody has to touch the puck for it to be icing, and it doesn't matter if the teams are at equal strength or a team is shorthanded.

Summing up, whatever rules you play by, keep in mind that you don't help your team if you continually get called for needless violations and end up in the penalty box.

Butting

Glossary

of Hockey Terms

Glossary

of Hockey Terms

Attacking zone—
> area from an opponent's blue line to goal line where the goal cage is located.

Backchecking—
> skating back toward your own goal to help out defensemen and goaltender while trying to regain the puck from the opposition.

Beat the defense—
> to move past the defenseman and in on the goaltender.

Blind pass—
> passing the puck without looking.

Blue line—

the line at each end of the rink that defines the attacking zone. These lines are also used to determine off sides. No attacking player may precede the puck over the defensive team's blue line.

Body check—

using your body (hip or shoulder) to stop an opponent.

Breakaway—

puck carrier skating in alone on goaltender with no opposing player between him and the net.

Checking—

defending against or guarding an opponent. Harassing an opposing skater with the aim of making him surrender the puck.

Clear puck—

keeping the puck away from own goal area.

Cover—

a defensive player covering an opponent closely in his own defensive end so that he can't receive a pass.

Crease—

the rectangular area marked off in front of each net.

Curved stick—

a stick with a hook in the blade as opposed to a flat stick.

Cutting—

crossing over skate stride when turning.

Defensive zone—

area from goal line to blue line where team's own goal cage is located.

Deflect—
to change the direction of the puck with stick or body.

Deke—
to fake a man out of position while carrying the puck.

Draw—
another way of saying face-off.

Dribble—
to move the puck from side to side or back and forth with the blade of your stick.

Drop pass—
to leave the puck for a trailing teammate to pick up.

Face-off—
the dropping of the puck between two players to start or re-sume play.

Feeding—
passing the puck.

Flip pass—
to lift the puck softly over an opponent's stick while making a pass.

Floater—
offensive player who slips behind the attacking defensemen looking for a breakaway. Also called sleeper or hanger.

Forechecking—
checking an opponent in his defensive zone as he attempts to start a play.

Freezing the puck—
pinning the puck against the boards with either your skate or your stick to force a stoppage in play and a face-off.

Get the jump—
to get a fast start on an opponent.

Hat trick—
three or more goals by a single player in one game.

Head-man—
a quick lead pass by a defenseman to a center or wing breaking into center ice.

Head-manning—
always advancing the puck to a teammate up ice.

Hip check—
to use your hip to knock an opponent off stride.

Icing the puck—
shooting the puck from behind the center red line across an opponent's goal line when both teams are skating at equal strength.

Neutral zone—
the center ice area between the blue lines.

Off side—
a violation called when an attacking player precedes the puck across the opponent's blue line.

Off-side pass—
a violation called when the puck is passed to a teammate across two or more lines.

On the fly—

changing players on the ice while play is going on.

Penalty killer—

a player whose job it is to use up time while a teammate is serving a penalty. The best penalty killers are fast skaters who can break up a power play.

Playmaker—

the player who sets up various plays and gives direction. Most often this is the center.

Points—

defenseman's position on the attacking blue line.

Poke check—

to make a sudden jab at the puck with your stick.

Power play—

the situation in which the team with a man advantage during the course of a penalty sends five men into the shorthanded team's defensive zone.

Puck—

the vulcanized rubber disk used in hockey.

Pulling the goaltender—

taking the goaltender off ice to replace him with a forward as an extra skater. This is a last-minute attempt to score a goal when a team is behind and the game is almost over.

Ragging—

retaining possession of the puck by clever stickhandling.

Rebound—

a shot that bounces off the goaltender or his equipment.

Red line—

the line that divides the ice surface in half.

Rush—

the situation in which a player or his team carries the puck into the opponent's defensive zone.

Save—

stop made by the goaltender.

Scramble—

players battling for the puck in close-range action.

Screen shot—

a shot through a group of players the goaltender is unable to see because of the men between himself and the shooter.

Shorthanded—

a team with a man in the penalty box that is skating one less man during the course of action.

Slap shot—

a shot in which the player winds up and slaps his stick at the puck.

Splitting the defense—

a puck carrier breaking through two defensemen.

Stick lie—

the angle between the blade and the shaft of the stick.

Stickhandling—

the art of carrying the puck with the stick.

Sweep check—

a sweeping motion, with stick flat on ice, that allows you to hook the puck away from an opponent.

Trailer—

player who follows his teammates, giving the impression that he is out of play, but then moves into position to take a drop pass.

Uncovered—

a player left unguarded in front of the net.

Index

Index

Illustrations are indicated by *italic* type.

137